BEST OF Jazz Piano

BY GENE RIZZO

ISBN 0-634-06010-4

HAL•LEONARD®
CORPORATION

7777 W. BLUEMOUND RD. P.O. BOX 13819 MILWAUKEE, WI 53213

Visit Hal Leonard ...
www.halleonard.com

D081431?

DEDICATION

To Joseph and Bernadette Ruggiero, who never judge and always praise.

PREFACE

A jazz pianist needs an unfettered imagination like a brain surgeon needs a chainsaw. His/her problem is not too little freedom of self-expression, but too much. What Maurice Ravel once called "the ability to dance in chains" seems particularly applicable to artists working in a largely improvised music. Here, then, is a survey of the styles and techniques used by eleven of jazz piano's best and most balletic chain dancers to help shine a light on a unique creative process that is sometimes unduly shrouded in mystery.

Gene Rizzo

DISCOGRAPHY

"It's Only a Paper Moon" – *After Midnight*
       Capitol 7243-5, 1956
"Come Rain or Come Shine" – *Portrait in Jazz*
       Original Jazz Classics OJCCD088, 1959
"How Deep Is the Ocean (How High Is the Sky)" – *Bill Evans Trio Live*
       Verve V68803, 1964
"In a Sentimental Mood" – *Moodsville 9*
       Original Jazz Classics OJCCD182-2, 1960
"Take the 'A' Train" – *Plays Ellington & Strayhorn*
       Columbia LP FC37639, 1981
"I'll Remember April" – *Concert by the Sea*
       Columbia CK40589, 1955
"There Is No Greater Love" – *At the Pershing*
       MCA-Chess CHD9108, 1958
"Speak Low" – *Happy Moods*
       Argo LP662, 1960
"St. Louis Blues" – *Duo with Hank Jones - Live in Tokyo*
       AMJ ABCJ-216, 1976
"Stompin' at the Savoy" – *An Evening with Two Grand Pianos*
       Little David LD1079, 1979
"No Moon at All" – *Back Home*
       Original Jazz Classics OJCCD971-2, 1976
"On a Clear Day (You Can See Forever)" – *The Good Life*
       Original Jazz Classics OJCCD627-2, 1973
"Caravan" – *The Giants*
       Original Jazz Classics OJCCD858-2, 1974
"Satin Doll" – *Jazz at the Musikverein*
       Verve 704-2, 1995
"Wrap Your Troubles in Dreams (And Dream Your Troubles Away)" – *Ten Fingers - One Voice*
       Arkadia 71602, 1996

CONTENTS

NAT "KING" COLE
(1917–1965)

In spite of his enormous success as a pop singer, Cole's credentials as a jazz pianist remain impeccable. Alabama-born and Chicago-bred, he began as a knock-off of Earl Hines but ultimately came upon a more laconic approach better suited to his temperate nature and velvety touch. His witty riffs and the sparse but effective use of his left hand provide the connecting link between the landmark styles of Teddy Wilson and Bud Powell. Jazz journalism is rife with glowing endorsements of his playing by many front rank pianists.

Cole revolutionized piano trio instrumentation in 1938 by using a guitarist in place of a drummer. Drummerless trios have since been implemented by such pianist/leaders as Art Tatum, Oscar Peterson, Andre Previn, and Diana Krall. By the early fifties, the demands of a chart-busting songbird eclipsed Cole's career as a pianist. The 1956 album *After Midnight*, his last hurrah as a jazz musician, showed that he was still capable of high-tier creativity.

IT'S ONLY A PAPER MOON

Lyric by Billy Rose and E.Y. Harburg
Music by Harold Arlen

Figure 1 – Intro

Cheerful two-measure riffs such as these were ingeniously threaded into many of Cole's solos. The A♭ (the final note in measures 2 and 6) changes to D and F in measures 4 and 8, respectively, serving as a kind of rhyming answer to the initial phrase. Trumpeter Harry "Sweets" Edison's tight harmon mute is in unison with the piano for the most part, lending an extra dimension of sassiness to the line.

Figure 2 – Solo (first 16 measures)

Although he wasn't the kind of cerebral player who obsesses over melodic cells, Cole often liked to confine his ideas within the general range of an interval established by a prominent figure. A pair of eighth notes outlining a 5th (C down to F) at the beginning of measure 1 set the boundary of all the melodic activity until the middle of measure 7. Similarly, the dual F notes on beat 4 of measure 12, followed by a sixteenth-note arpeggio ending on F in the lower octave, stake out new intervallic territory. The swinging line extending from measures 13–16 observe the octave limit, except for a few errant middle C notes.

Figure 3 – Solo (bridge and last 8 measures)

The pianist, not surprisingly, chooses to riff his two-measure trades with Edison's trumpet on the bridge. Cole cleverly paraphrases measures 1 and 2 in measures 5 and 6. The glissando that begins in measure 12 is a Cole stock-in-trade that found favor with two of the pianist's most devoted champions: Red Garland and Ahmad Jamal.

BILL EVANS
(1929–1980)

Evans is the most influential jazz pianist since Bud Powell. At the height of the hard bop vogue (late 1950s), when far too many pianists were shamelessly recycling the same gospel and funk-addled licks, Evans's lyricism and thoughtful introspection provided an attractive stylistic alternative—one destined for a long shelf life. As the hard bop "preachers" went the obsolescent way of blacksmiths, hangmen, and chimneysweeps, the twenty-something from Plainfield, New Jersey gathered a growing army of imitators. Evansistas keep surfacing even among the most recent young lions of jazz piano.

A distinguished sideman before he mounted a solo career, Evans participated in the Miles Davis watershed album *Kind of Blue* in 1958. He was given too little credit for his invaluable services as the session's co-arranger and composer. Later, as a truly inventive trio leader, he railed against the traditional use of bass and drums as mere keepers of windshield wiper time. He encouraged his sidemen to take a more pro-active role in the scaffolding of the music—a pioneering concept as common now as the older paradigm. Evans fought a losing battle with drug addiction and died, tragically, at 51.

COME RAIN OR COME SHINE

Words by Johnny Mercer
Music by Harold Arlen

Figure 4 - Head (first 16 measures)

This great Harold Arlen standard is well suited for vocalists with a half-spoken, half-sung style (like Frank Sinatra). But the song's profusion of repeated notes makes it less than ideal for piano interpretation. Evans sidesteps the problem of jackhammering the A in measures 1 and 2 by alternating it with little flourishes built on lower neighboring notes. In measures 5 and 6, the droning A notes appear mostly on tied upbeats, as though in protest to their insistence. Overall, the melody is paraphrased but easily recognizable.

Harmonically, the chords are densely clustered. The upper partials (9ths, 11ths, 13ths) often appear in the lower areas of the voicings (e.g. the Em11b5 on beat 1 of measure 2, the altered A7 on beat 3 of the same measure, and the Db13 on beat 3 of measure 7).

Figure 5 – Head (last 16 measures)

The pesky A melody note is ignored entirely in measures 1 and 2. Evans uses Arlen's recurring B notes in measures 5 and 6, doubling them with a vengeance in the lower octave of block chords. The ascending 10ths in measure 8 are a favorite device of this pianist when approaching a climax. Measure 9 begins the high drama of the song's last section. Here Evans pays homage to Debussy and Ravel, composers whose harmonic practices play such an integral part in his work.

Figure 6 – Solo Chorus (first 8 measures)

Evans's right hand has covered a range of almost three octaves in the first three measures—and done so with genuinely melodic ideas. Measures 5–7 are more sparsely noted; he has found a minor 2nd (B and C) that he exploits on beat 2 of measure 5. He playfully repeats it four more times in different rhythmic locations; the last time is rendered as two consecutive notes on beat 2 of measure 7. The momentary fascination with the half-step grind is over by measure 8.

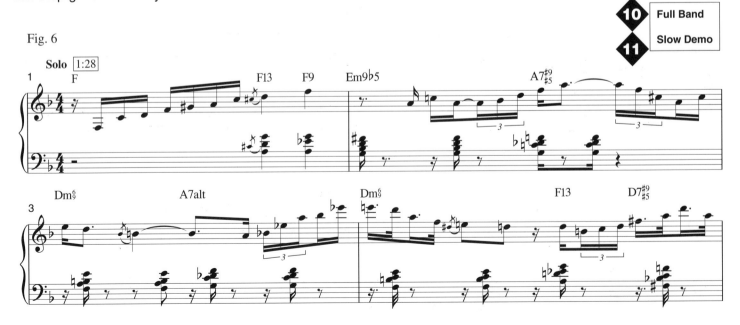

Figure 7 – Solo Chorus (second 8 measures)

Sixteenth-note triplets followed by a pair of sixteenths are common in Evans's ballad playing. They appear no less than seven times in this section. A particularly characteristic application is heard in measure 5 where all but the last of four such units are tied together.

HOW DEEP IS THE OCEAN (HOW HIGH IS THE SKY)

Words and Music by Irving Berlin

Figure 8 – Head (first 16 measures)

No semblance of the original melody appears here. The shift from Cm in the first eight to A♭ thereafter is the only suggestion that distinguishes the A from the B sections in the head of this A–B–A–C evergreen. Rootless left hand voicings abound. They often join the right hand to reinforce pivotal notes in the lines. The pianist is not shy about using ♯9 chords where applicable.

Figure 9 – Head (last 8 measures)

This is the most explicit reference to the original melody in the entire presentation of the head. The block chords (four-part chords with the top voice doubled an octave lower) heard from measures 3–8 are quite a frequently used Evans device.

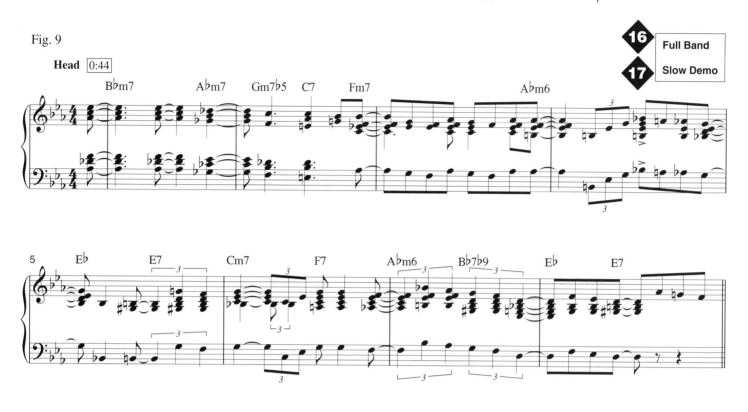

Figure 10 – Second Solo Chorus (first 8 measures)

Unlike his imitators, Evans executed stretches of two-handed unison rhythms such as these (measures 1–4) without ever sounding ham-fisted. Measures 5–8 bring out the double-time bebopper in him. Evans had a commanding technique but used it in small doses.

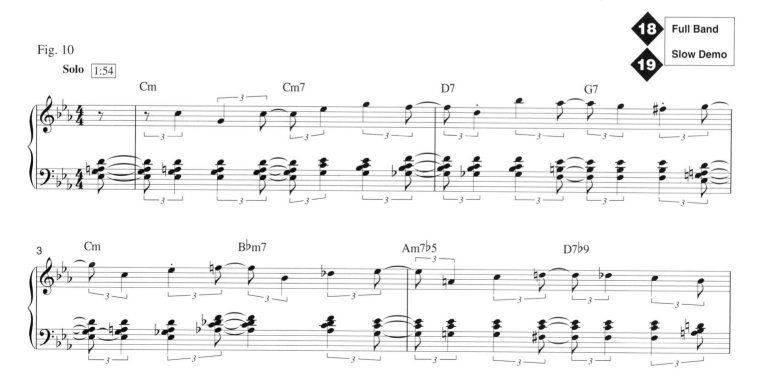

Figure 11 – Second Solo Chorus (last 16 measures)

Triplets give measures 3–8 a particularly swinging momentum. Whether on strong beats (1 and 3) or weak beats (2 and 4), they gracefully moderate the otherwise eighth-noted lines. Measures 10–15 constitute another double-time bop fable. In measure 16, the general flurry of sixteenth notes ends in relaxed triplets.

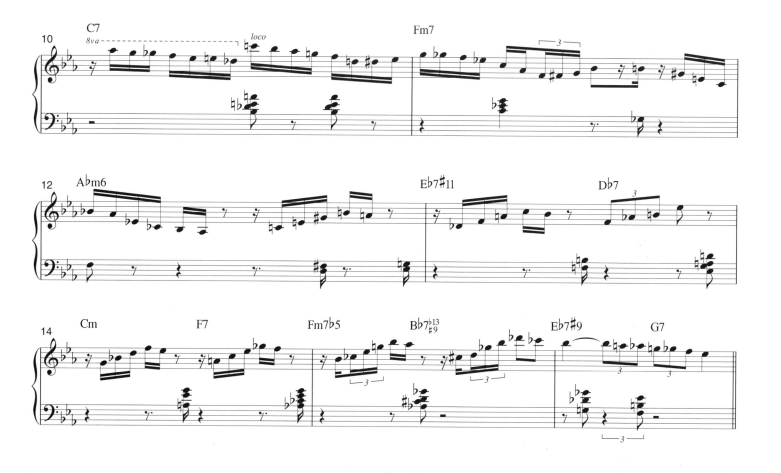

Figure 12 – Reprise (last section and ending)

After extensive block chording, Evans modulates by way of a ii–V in measure 10 (Dm7–G7) to the key of C major. Measures 11 and 12 find him backpeddling to the home key of E♭ through a sequence of chords joined by major 3rd relationships (Cmaj7#11–A♭maj7#11–Emaj7#11). In measure 13, the scales of E♭ major and its relative C minor cap one of Evans's finest performances of the mid-sixties.

Fig. 12

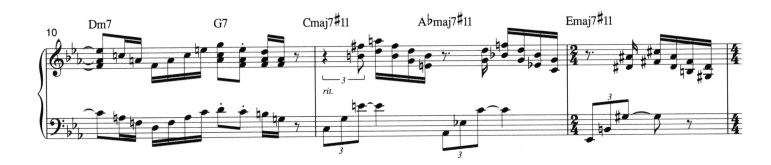

TOMMY FLANAGAN
(1930–2001)

Flanagan was too busy as an A-list sideman and singers' accompanist to launch a solo career until he reached middle age. The ex-Detroiter was relatively unknown when he emigrated to Manhattan in 1956. Appearing in the late fifties on two milestone recordings (*Saxophone Colossus* with Sonny Rollins and *Giant Steps* with John Coltrane) failed to lure Flanagan toward the center of the stage. He continued to work in a subordinate role with many iconic tenor saxophonist/leaders. After long stints as a musical director with Ella Fitzgerald and Tony Bennett in the sixties and early seventies, the combined efforts of record producers, concert promoters, and club owners finally convinced him to show his wares as a worthy entity in his own right.

A distinctive approach to harmony and line defies the frequent characterization of Flanagan and other unique Motor City pianists (Hank Jones, Barry Harris, Roland Hanna) as little more than a mid-western gaggle of Bud Powell wannabes. The so-called Detroit School, it turns out, is a geographical rubric at best.

IN A SENTIMENTAL MOOD

By Duke Ellington

Figure 13 – First Solo Chorus (first 16 measures)

One of Flanagan's heroes, Teddy Wilson, is never far from his thoughts. The scalar passagework, the sixteenth and dotted eighth-note couplings (particularly on beat 1 of measure 6), and even the almost fox trot tempo suggest Wilson's ballad style. Flanagan's own imprint is distinguishable from the older master's by, among other things, his fondness for higher partials in the melodic line (e.g. the 9ths in measures 3, 4, 9, 14, and 16, and G, the recurring 11th in measure 10).

Fig. 13

Figure 14 – First Solo Chorus (bridge)

Lush harmony hides the pedestrian I–vi–ii–V sequence of the first four measures very well. Beats 3 and 4 of measure 4 stray from the pattern's expected A♭7 (the V in this key of D♭) with a tritone substitution chord (D9). Measure 1 delivers most of the bridge's original melodic phrase in only half the time. A clever truncation, it would normally have spanned the entire measure. At measure 8, the pianist evades the familiar sheet music pick-up built on the F pentatonic scale (F–G–A–C–D) that precedes the next section. The evasion is a consistent practice throughout this performance until the ending.

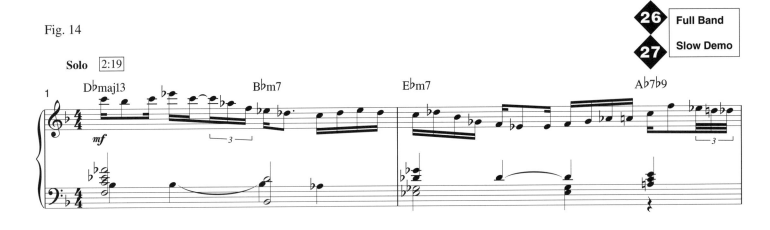

Fig. 14

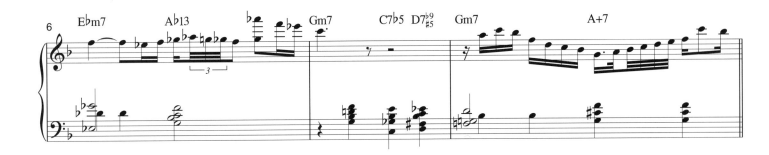

Figure 15 – First Solo Chorus (last 8 measures)

In measure 4, Flanagan's grace notes accent the first two couplings of sixteenth notes followed by dotted eighths. The third and fourth pairings make good melodic use of a ♭9th and a ♯5th. Measure 7 introduces triads, some of which contain altered higher partials.

Fig. 15

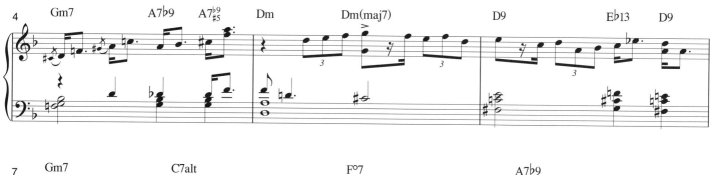

Figure 16 – Second Solo Chorus (bridge)

Flanagan calls on his D9 substitution again in measure 4, while continuing the triadic sequence begun in the previous measure. Bare 4ths, 5ths, and a pair of closely voiced four-part chords in measure 5 are welcome new elements in the improvisation. The pianist uses rootless left hand voicing less frequently than chords with well-anchored roots.

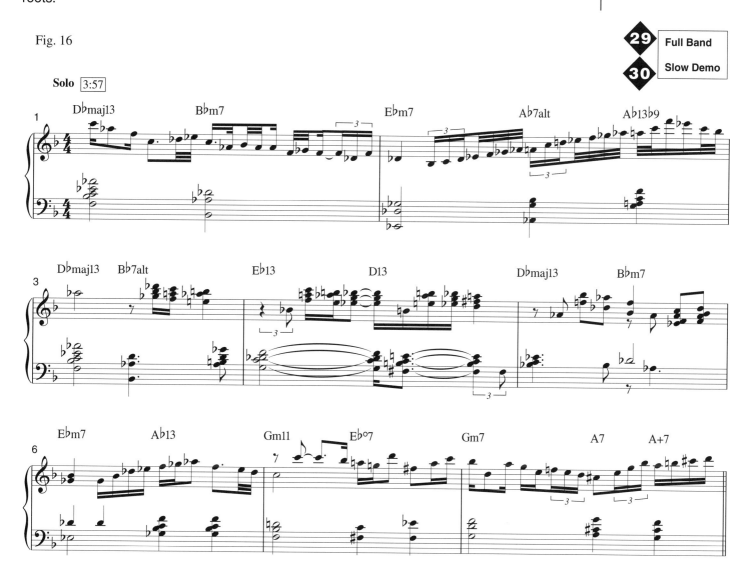

Figure 17 – Recap (last 8 measures and ending)

The recap is fairly literal. Flanagan gets Wilsonian again in the quarter-note triplets of measure 6, lining a D9 with two passing chords. A false cadence arrives not on an F chord but a richly voiced D♭13 (measure 8). Flanagan finally incorporates the pentatonic pick-up phrase he has been eluding in the final measures.

JIMMY ROWLES
(1918–1996)

Rowles was the sole white member of Lester Young's band at the Trouville Club in downtown Los Angeles in 1942. Originally from Spokane, Washington, his earlier aspirations to play professional tennis were all but forgotten when he settled in the City of Angels. Following his discharge from the army in 1945, he plied his trade in the two arenas that would define his career for nearly thirty years: singers' accompanist and studio musician. Rowles was, at one time or another, the power behind the thrones of Billie Holiday, Ella Fitzgerald, Carmen McRae, Sarah Vaughan, and Tony Bennett. His many contributions to film soundtracks include the boogie-woogie calliope part on Henry Mancini's *Baby Elephant Walk.* When Hollywood's music departments began using cost-effective synthesizers in the early seventies, the pianist moved his base of operations to New York City.

Rowles's appearance as a soloist at the 1973 Newport Jazz Festival was a watershed. A witty, personal style previously known to only an inner circle of musicians advanced from the background to the foreground. His subsequent recordings as a soloist/trio leader are uncommonly good, although his creative energies are sometimes wasted on long forgotten songs few listeners know well enough to appreciate. His own catalog of compositions boasts the tuneful little masterpiece "The Peacocks."

TAKE THE "A" TRAIN

Words and Music by Billy Strayhorn

Figure 18 – Intro

The familiar ducal intro is replicated, but Rowles signs his own name in measures 7 and 8 with a I–♭II–♭VI–V chordal sequence.

Figure 19 – Head (first 8 measures)

The melody's first four measures are abstracted by long tied notes and supported with close-voiced, low register chords. (Rowles was fonder of the instrument's basement than other pianists.) A bit of riffing and a pair of major 2nds ascending chromatically complete the section.

Figure 20 – Head (bridge)

Rowles withholds A, the major 3rd of the Fmaj7, until the upbeat of beat 3 in measure 2. He is less reticent to add the crucial note to the rich harmony of measures 3 and 4. His left hand deftly comps for his right. It doesn't always deploy chords; single notes suffice in the virtually two-part counterpoint of measures 7 and 8.

Fig. 20

Figure 21 – First Solo Chorus (first 16 measures)

The absence of scalar ideas is noteworthy. Rowles's lines have genuinely melodic contours built around primary chord members. His left hand remains a basso profundo. It states an interesting Db7b5 in measure 6 and repeats it in measure 14. The right hand prepares to enter the subdominant key of F (measures 15 and 16) via a C7, the secondary dominant. The deed is done with a harmonically self-sufficient phrase.

ERROLL GARNER
(1921–1977)

Pittsburgh was lousy with great piano players in the first half of the twentieth century. Earl Hines spearheaded a homegrown daisy chain, which included Mary Lou Williams, Ahmad Jamal, Billy Strayhorn, Dodo Marmarosa, Horace Parlan, and, arguably the greatest of them, Erroll Garner. Despite an inability to read music and a scattershot knowledge of musical mechanics, Garner became one of the most loved musicians in jazz.

His party-hearty style, with its infectious rhythm guitar-like left hand, first attracted attention on New York's famed 52nd Street in the final days of WWII. He held his own against Art Tatum and Bud Powell, the street's top competitors. By the mid-fifties, Garner, the composer of the hit ballad "Misty," had accumulated a vast constituency, including many fans whom otherwise professed to dislike jazz. He frequently appeared on TV variety shows. In the late fifties he signed an exclusive contract with the classical music impresario, Sol Hurok, to appear in prestigious concert halls. Record producers, hat in hand, continually dogged him to sign on with their label. Amazingly, for all his success, Garner never settled for less than the highest standards of creativity.

I'LL REMEMBER APRIL

Words and Music by Pat Johnson, Don Raye and Gene De Paul

Figure 22 – Intro

The sputtering right hand repetitions of a chord cluster suggest a message in Morse code. By measure 12, enough F and A♭ notes have been sounded in both hands to identify the prevailing tonality as being that of F minor. Measures 21–22 bring back the Morse code motif. When the altered C7 chords begin on the second beat of measure 26, they serve as the dominant for the key that has been Garner's objective all along: F major.

Fig. 22

Figure 23 – Head (first 16 measures)

The left hand performs double duty as a harmonic provider and quasi-rhythm guitar part. Octaves thickened by rich inner voices throw the melody into high relief against the accompaniment. Garner sounds, as usual, virtually self-contained; the rhythm section could just as well have phoned in their parts. The pianist indulges his penchant for a repeated chord introduced by a half-step lower neighbor in measures 9–10.

Figure 24 – Head (bridge)

Tremolos, one of Garner's most cheerful devices, stimulate the long sustained notes in measures 3 and 9. We met measure 5's repeated chords with half-step lower neighbors in Fig. 23. Good hand independence is required to bring off the opposing rhythms of measures 13–15. The final measure features some surprising voice leading; the lowest note in the G9 (A, the 9th) approaches the root of the C13 by way of a minor 3rd. It's not your garden variety V of V root movement, but it's convincing nonetheless.

Fig. 24

Figure 25 – First Solo Chorus (bridge)

Garner's eighth-note lines are truly an embarrassment of melodic riches. The ideas, with a few range modifications, would make an excellent five-way sax section soli. The pianist owes a greater debt to the dance bands he listened to as a teenager in the East Liberty section of Pittsburgh than is generally known. Measures 13–14 are more pianistic. Earl Hines, another Garner influence, enjoyed playful octave leaps like these.

Fig. 25

Figure 26 – First Solo Chorus (last 16 measures)

The many passing tones in the line from measures 1–4 rebel against the unchanging F chord. Garner appears to be more compliant with the restraints of Fm7 in the next four measures; his note choices focus on primary chord members. Measure 16's majestic chord cluster is worthy of a McCoy Tyner.

Fig. 26

44 Full Band
45 Slow Demo

AHMAD JAMAL
(1930–)

Jamal was playing Lizst etudes at age 11—chopsy fare for the future best-selling recording artist who made his bones as a master of economy and understatement. By the late 1950s, his affiliations with classical piano literature were replaced by the altissimo register twitterings, pregnant silences, and rubato-like phrasing of a remarkable jazz style. Except for occasional echoes of his fellow Pittsburghers, Earl Hines and Erroll Garner, Jamal's approach was sui generis. The Chess recording *Ahmad Jamal at the Pershing* (1958) was a surprising hit given its piano trio instrumentation and the less-is-more credo of its leader. The success was repeated on three more chart-busting albums. Their fan base included no less a seminal figure than Miles Davis.

Jamal has not allowed his unique style to slip into self-parody. Some disenchanted admirers have, consequently, left the fold. Far notier these days, the pianist's earlier Lizstian proclivities have come full circle. But enough silences, bird twitterings, and floating phrases prevail to confirm his trademark. An artist for whom a songwriter's melody was never Holy Writ, Jamal's treatment of standards has become increasingly abstract.

THERE IS NO GREATER LOVE

Words by Marty Symes
Music by Isham Jones

Figure 27 – Head (first 16 measures)

The eight-measure melody is given two sharply contrasting presentations: measures 1–8 in single notes and measures 9–16 in close-voiced chords. The first three notes of measure 1 would have been played as quarter-note pick-ups in a more traditional performance. Jamal belatedly concedes to that tradition in measure 9. In measures 15–16 he leaves the turnarounds to the rhythm section.

Figure 28 – Head (bridge)

The repetitious melody, however freely phrased, clearly outlines an arpeggiated E7 to an Am7. Vertical chords are reserved for the last two measures. They appear in a pyramid formation (measure 7) and stacked in 4ths (measure 8). The latter is a reprise of the pick-up cited in Fig. 27.

Figure 29 – Solo (first 16 measures)

Jamal finds fresh configurations for the original melody (measures 1–4). In measures 9–13, he has taken a shine to the would-be folk song "Where the Wild Goose Goes," which he quotes sequentially while the left hand traffics in upbeats.

SPEAK LOW

Words by Ogden Nash
Music by Kurt Weill

Figure 30 – Head (first 16 measures)

Jamal is more faithful than usual to the composer's melody but veers intriguingly off-message in measures 12–16. The head is cast in stop-time for the most part. Rootless voicings allow the mighty Israel Crosby, Jamal's bassist at the time, to furnish the anchors. The G pick-up notes in measure 16 refuse to yield ground to their upper and lower neighbors.

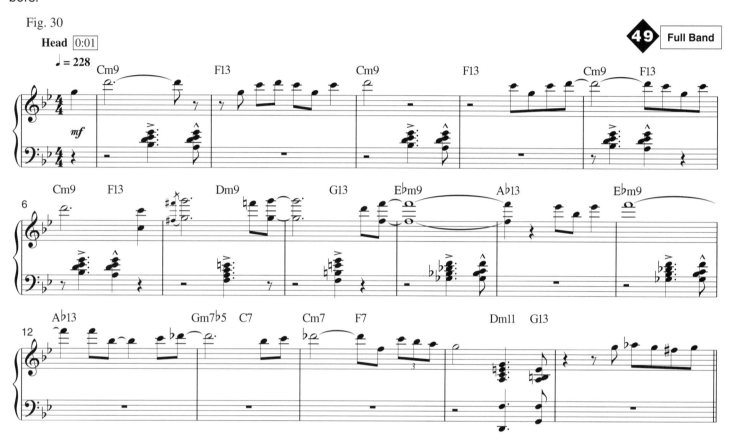

Figure 31 – First Solo Chorus (bridge)

Only Jamal would risk implementing the grinding left-hand cluster in measures 1 and 2. The ♭5th of the V chord (F7) in measure 8 is a more consonant modification.

Figure 32 – 1st Solo Chorus (bridge)

Jamal, as many recordings will show, is not always an improviser in the usual sense. He is sometimes more inclined to embellish the head where others would ignore it entirely. Measures 1–2 and 5–6 are typical of such paraphrasings. The Gb13 tremolos of measures 3–4 are a momentary salute to Earl Hines. The whole tone scale lick on F (F–G–A–B–C#–Eb) in measure 8 nods to Erroll Garner.

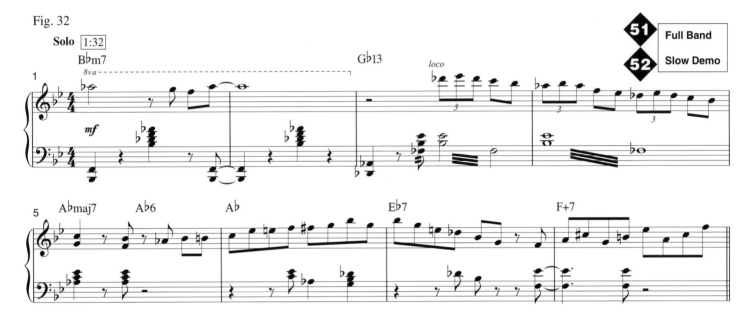

Figure 33 – 2nd Solo Chorus (first 16 measures)

The two ascending arpeggios spaced an octave apart in measure 6 are almost twins, except for the third note of each unit. Jamal uses ties in measures 9–12 to relieve the monotony of the ii–V chords. The first four eighth notes of measure 14 begin an F diminished scale (F–Gb–Ab–A–B–C–D–Eb) that's aborted on the third beat. The last measure's octave shake borrows again from the Earl Hines/Erroll Garner jazz piano manual.

JOHN LEWIS
(1920–2001)

Lewis was a criminally underrated pianist. There are enough fine moments in his discography, however, to warrant a reconsideration of the matter. Although not an improviser in the feral, scorched-earth vein of an Oscar Peterson or a Bud Powell, Lewis brought the refreshing virtues of grace and classical discipline to jazz playing.

Originally from La Grange, Illinois, Lewis was raised in Albuquerque, New Mexico. Military service during WWII aborted his studies at the University of New Mexico, where he had taken on a double major of music and anthropology. He was discharged in 1945. His long quadruple threat career (pianist, composer, arranger, teacher) began with Dizzy Gillespie's big band (1946–47). It continued with many other giants, most notably in the company of the Modern Jazz Quartet (1952–74 and again after its re-formation 1982–95). A revered academic, Lewis headed the faculty at the Lenox School of Jazz in Lenox, Massachusetts during the late fifties and taught at Harvard (1975) and the City College of New York (1975–82). He was also the musical director of the Monterey Jazz Festival from 1958–82. His voluminous catalog of compositions includes the classic "Django."

ST. LOUIS BLUES

Words and Music by W.C. Handy

Figure 34 – First Solo Chorus

Lewis's blues are a shade lighter than most—closer to cornflower blue. Note how he sanitizes the funky E♭ notes over the C chords of measures 3 and 7 by placing them on upbeats. The solo is not exclusively right-handed for want of an able left hand; Lewis is giving his duo partner, Hank Jones, some comping room.

Figure 35 – Second Solo Chorus

Measure 3 recycles measure 1 more succinctly. Measure 6's relationship to measure 4 is less obvious; the lines are different melodically but almost identical in rhythm. Lewis's sense of order is typically cogent, riding on an implied double-time groove.

Figure 36 – Third Solo Chorus

The solo is gathering momentum. We now have more of an eighth-note line and some Charlie Parker-ish passing tones. The grace notes in measures 6–8 effectively italicize primary chord members.

Figure 37 – Fourth Solo Chorus

Riffing keeps the solo moving forward (measures 1–3). Lewis was a master at building clearly terraced solos. The tension begins to relax at measure 9 where the solo draws to an inexorable conclusion with the first of four phrases, three of which contain a prominent semi-tone motif.

STOMPIN' AT THE SAVOY

By Benny Goodman, Edgar Sampson and Chick Webb

Figure 38 – First Solo Chorus (first 16 measures)

Here is Lewis's best folk song bag; his lines over the changes of this swing era warhorse are as rustic as a dust bowl farmhouse. The last eight measures mirror the first eight, whose melody, except for some maverick E♮ notes, strictly observes the key of D♭ (D♭–E♭–F–G♭–A♭–B♭–C–D♭). Occasionally, Lewis calls on his left hand for octave reinforcement.

Figure 39 – 1st Solo Chorus (bridge)

Lewis is back to his bebop roots, although few Bud Powell acolytes would be satisfied with the elegant simplicity of measures 3–7. This pianist was loathe to flaunt his considerable technique.

Fig. 39

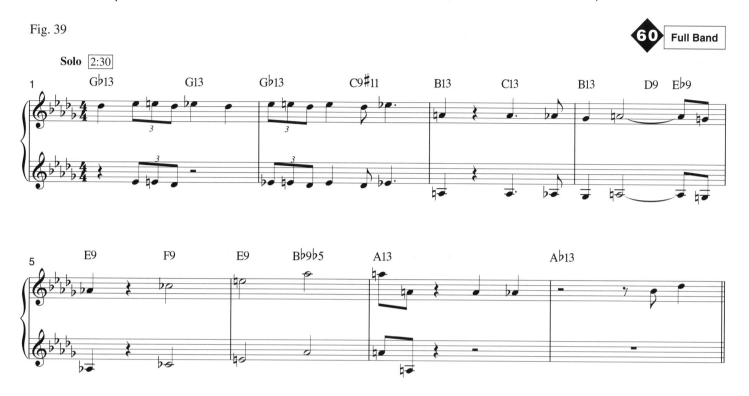

Figure 40 – 1st Solo Chorus (last 8 measures)

The entire section recalls the limpid phrases of Lester Young, whom Lewis channeled from time to time. Measures 4 and 5 are direct "Prez" quotes chapter and verse.

Fig. 40

PHINEAS NEWBORN
(1931–1989)

Newborn was raised in Memphis, Tennessee, a city he left under protest when Count Basie convinced him to do so. Basie was part of a determined effort, together with the Willard Alexander booking agency and jazz promoter John Hammond, to set Newborns's appreciable wares before New York's most demanding jazz fans. The pianist came prepared—his classical trained virtuosity, vivid harmonic imagination, and driving swing well in place. After a successful engagement at Basin Street East, he changed his base of operations (1956) and immediately became an Apple frontrunner on recordings and live appearances.

A move to Los Angeles in 1961 marked a slow, steady decline in Newborn's health and career. He fell victim to an emotional illness and was admitted to Camarillo State Hospital. When he returned to playing, many of his former advocates in the jazz press had a change of heart. They accused him of freely indulging in shallow displays of technique. Newborn occasionally reined in his fleet fingers, but not often enough to make peace with the superchops police. The recordings he is rumored to have made in 1987 of sonatas by the eccentric Russian composer Alexander Scriabin suggest he may have once considered a career change to the concert hall, where weapons-grade hands are more appreciated.

NO MOON AT ALL

By Dave Mann and Redd Evans

Figure 41 – Intro

Newborn introduces an innocuous figure (measures 1 and 2). In measures 3–5, a chord which would otherwise be an A♭maj9 were it not for the discordant inclusion of D♭ beats out a catchy rhythmic motif. Measure 9 embroiders a G♭maj7 chord with triplets borrowed from the G♭ Lydian mode (G♭–A♭–B♭–C–D♭–E♭–F–G♭). Another grinding chord perched on no less catchy a rhythmic motif than the previous one is heard from measure 11 to the intro's end. Its G♭ tonic leads to the main key of Fm by simply descending a half step.

Figure 42 – Head (first 9 measures)

Erroll Garner's influence on Newborn became increasingly obvious with the passing years. Measures 1–6 demonstrate that by 1996, when this recording was made, Newborn had adapted enough of a rhythm guitar-like left hand to please the most die-hard Garnerian. The false cadence on a D♭ chord (measure 7) and the half-step harmonic scheme that follow, however, backpedal to F minor in ways unique to Newborn.

Fig. 42

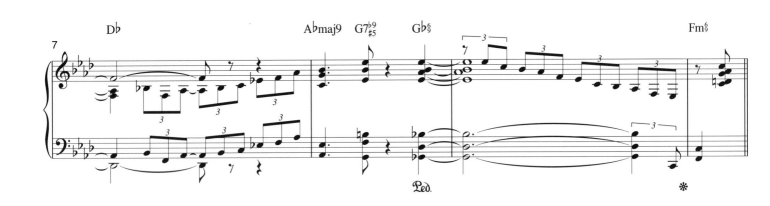

Figure 43 – Head (bridge)

Garner is referenced again, including the clipped chords on the upbeats of measures 2 and 4, which fill in the windows between phrases. An effective resource, much like punchy brass figures in a big band chart, this is a device pianists too rarely use. Even Newborn, who is more orchestrally oriented than others, was given to playing fills in melodic snippets in previous years.

Figure 44 – Solo Chorus (second 8 measures)

Newborn opens up the color range with an expansive foray into the outer regions of the changes. Full chords reinforce melodic ideas couched in octaves and 5ths. The amen cadence (sub-dominant to tonic) in measure 6 lends an interesting gospel flavor as the tension relaxes.

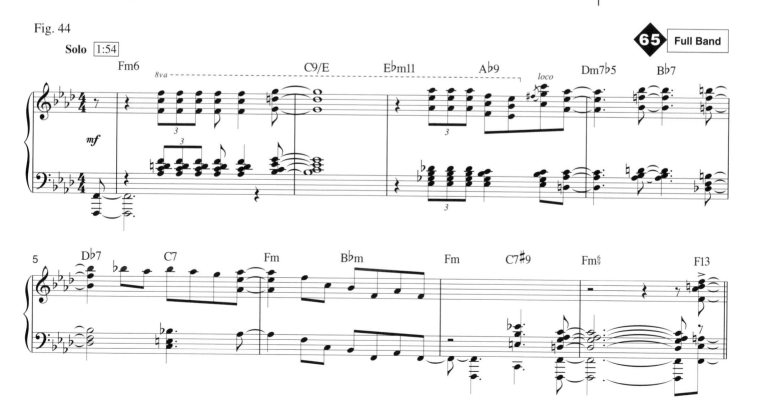

Figure 45 – Solo (bridge)

Here are the forbidding Newborn passages in double octaves that, as one critic so aptly put it, "make other pianists weep."

OSCAR PETERSON
(1925–)

There has never been any question about ranking Peterson in jazz piano's top tier. His fame rewards a creative brilliance indicated in the earliest stages of his career. In 1949, Norman Granz, the founder of Jazz at the Philharmonic concerts, was so overwhelmed when he heard the then young Canadian playing at the Alberta Lounge in Montreal he succeeded in committing him to a Carnegie Hall debut. Gotham's enthusiastic response to Granz's "discovery" has since been replicated in clubs and concert venues worldwide for more than half a century.

Peterson's recordings are as popular as they are numberless. Whether in trio or solo piano sessions, his playing is technically pristine, harmonically colorful, and buoyed by a contagious, swinging beat. His style cannot be mistaken for anyone else's, but traces of former idols Art Tatum and Nat Cole still linger in tribute at times. After a paralyzing stroke in 1993, which necessitated two grueling years of physical therapy, Peterson made a comeback and reclaimed most of his former glory as a true jazz giant.

ON A CLEAR DAY (YOU CAN SEE FOREVER)

Words by Alan Jay Lerner
Music by Burton Lane

Figure 46 – Head (pick-up and first 16 measures)

Composer Burton Lane's opening eight-measure strain, built mostly on a B♭maj9 arpeggio (B♭–D–F–A–C) in reverse, is fair game for a classic Peterson makeover. The pianist remains true to the original melody while tinkering with its rhythmic profile (the sixteenth-note triplet and eighth-note pairing on beat 3 of measure 2, the added C and A in measure 3, and the mini arpeggio in measure 4). Peterson prefers rhythmic modification to actual pitch distortion when outlining a head. The only significant deviation from the line is the long-held F in measure 13, but even that begins after the "true" C note has had its say.

Figure 47 – Head (bridge)

As is his want on bridges, Peterson allows himself freer rein. The half-step chord movement lends more animation than is generally heard on this tune in measures 1 and 2. There is a bit of riffing (measure 5), a well placed Db blue note (measure 6), and a Bbm chord does its funky best to replace an F7 on beat 1 of the last measure.

Figure 48 – Head (last 16 measures)

Peterson's orchestral side here is at full tilt. The melody, reinforced in octaves and 5ths, leaves the meat of the harmony to the left hand. The latter's voicings are wide open, as opposed to the usual practice of other pianists who generally use leaner, close-position chords in this style.

Figure 49 – Third Solo Chorus (first 16 measures)

Riffing triplets are virtually O.P.'s calling card (measures 1 and 2). Measure 8 begins a cascade of double-time ideas effortlessly executed. The out of key ii–V substitution chords (measure 14) are a tasty change-up for the expected D♭°7 before we are referred back to the standard changes.

Fig. 49

50

CARAVAN
Words and Music by Duke Ellington, Irving Mills and Juan Tizol

Figure 50 – First Solo Chorus (first 16 measures)

This is romping, high-octane bebop; few pianists in 1974 (the year this was recorded) could have resisted cramming every modal scale they knew into this section's twelve-measure stretch of C7 harmony. Quarter-note rests (measure 8) momentarily halt an eighth-note juggernaut that by measure 15 ends on the 5th of the chord—one of this artist's favorite cadential devices.

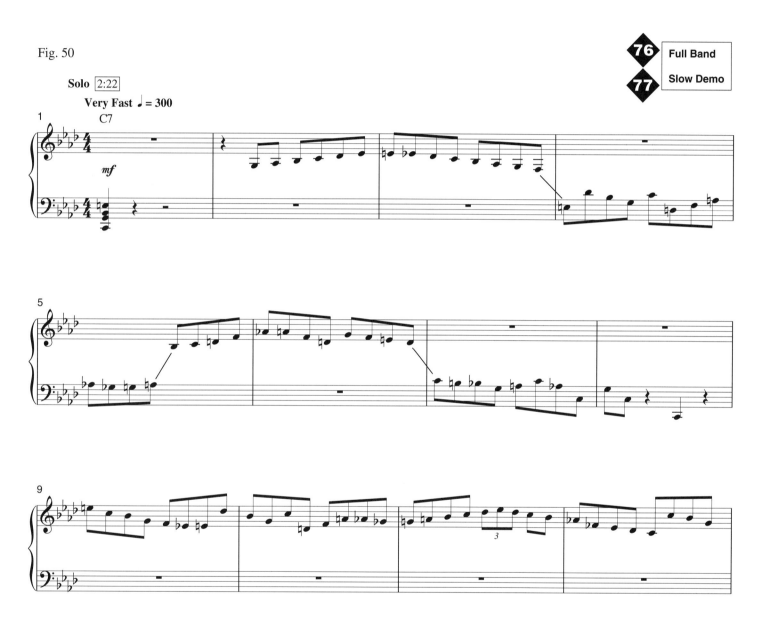

Figure 51 – First Solo Chorus (bridge)

The downbeat eighth notes on beats 1 and 3 of measures 1 and 2 herald a repeated figure. (Peterson's idols, Art Tatum, Teddy Wilson, and Nat Cole plied similar effective, but technically undemanding, licks). The remaining measures are far less hand-friendly; the lines roar through the cycle of 5ths ahead. Once C7 is reclaimed (measure 15), the keys of C and D major are briefly joined. A perky C+ arpeggio rounds off the section.

Fig. 51

78 Full Band

79 Slow Demo

Figure 52 – First Solo Chorus (last 16 measures)

Peterson's melodic ideas for the stubbornly anchored C7 chord appear to be inexhaustible. Only measures 4–6 are inclined toward arpeggiation. The line beginning on measure 13 ends on B♭, the dramatic 11th of the prevailing Fm chord.

Fig. 52

ANDRE PREVIN
(1929–)

In 1939, Previn was a budding virtuoso and a ten-year-old refugee from war-torn Europe. His parents, originally Berliners, took the advice of a relative who worked as a film cutter at MGM and fled with their precocious son to Los Angeles. Young Previn's legit background (the Berlin and Paris Conservatories) soon proved useful for odd jobs in MGM's music department. By age sixteen, he advanced from orchestrating staff composers' sketches to scoring entire films under his own title. A growing fascination with the styles of Art Tatum and Fats Waller sparked his first recordings as a jazz artist. Ultimately, Previn was managing a dual career and distinguishing himself in both. His recorded jazz treatment of "My Fair Lady" (1957) went gold, even as his arranging skills earned well deserved oscars for the lavish film musicals *Gigi* (1958), *Porgy and Bess* (1959), and, yet again, *My Fair Lady* (1964).

In the mid-sixties, Previn made a clean break with Hollywood and jazz to conduct world-class orchestras in symphonic repertoire. When in the late eighties he found that his jazz muse was dissatisfied with only being called upon for home recreation, the pianist took action. He cleared his schedule to allow for occasional recordings and public appearances with bassist Ray Brown and guitarist Mundell Lowe. More recently he has been working in a duo with virtuoso bassist David Finck. Still a brilliant, if part-time jazz musician, Previn is now the musical director of the Oslo Philharmonic.

SATIN DOLL

By Duke Ellington

Figure 53 – Intro and First 8 Measures

Previn has achieved the near impossible here—a fresh slant on a familiar lounge lizard anthem. Softly droning quarter notes lend a mysterioso quality to the ii–V intro. Quarter notes continue to dominate in the first 4 measures of the chorus. The major chord substitution for the standard Dm7 in measures 1 and 2 is unexpected, but a far greater shock occurs when a B7/F thumbs its nose at Em7 in measures 3 and 4.

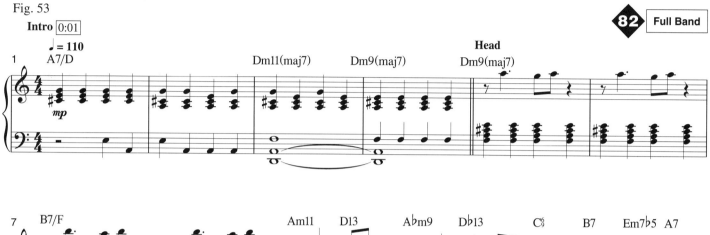

Figure 54 – Head (bridge)

Harmonic adventures are put on hold for a straightforward bridge rendering more in keeping with conversation over cocktails. Previn uses the ascending and descending triad fills (measures 3 and 7) Billy Strayhorn put in his famous chart for Duke Ellington's band.

Figure 55 – Head (last 8 measures with two-measure extension)

After a restless two-measure interlude, the A section is recalled with even more ambiguous harmony than before. The true melody is never heard in the right hand's eerie, high register 3rds; only the rhythmic profile confirms its identity. In measures 5 and 6, the B7/F, with its plangent minor 9th interval between the outer voices (F–F♯), persists in replacing Em7.

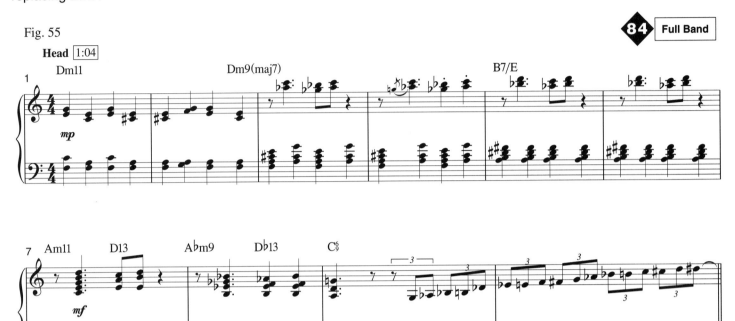

Figure 56 – First Solo Chorus (first 16 measures)

The solo unfolds in fitful rhythmic outbursts; Previn is no garden-variety bebopper hog-tied to eighth-note ideas. Although he has finally accepted the conventional chord changes, Previn shows a clear preference for their compound intervals (9ths, 11ths, 13ths). Measure 11 makes effective use of 9ths and 11ths in two phrases, the second of which subtly paraphrases the first.

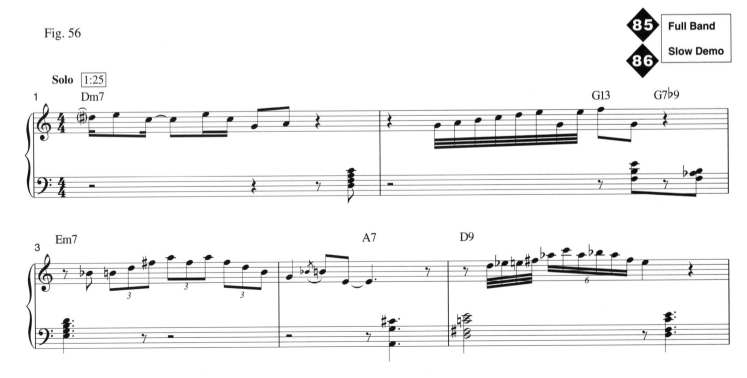

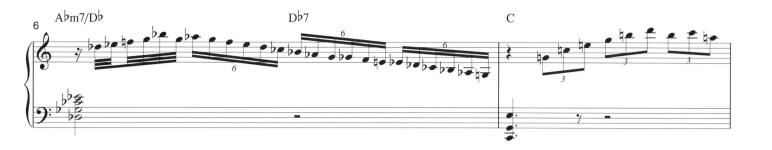

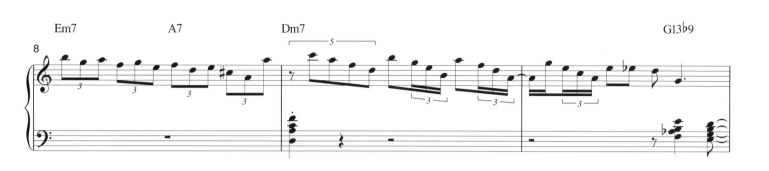

BILLY TAYLOR
(1921–)

Born in North Carolina, Taylor grew up in Washington, DC. His belief in the value of education surfaced early. He earned a bachelor of music degree from Virginia State College before taking on the other young guns of New York's 52nd Street. A gig with Ben Webster at the Three Deuces (1944) led straightaway to stints with more heavy hitters, including Stuff Smith, Billie Holiday, Dizzy Gillespie, and Machito's Afro-Cuban band. In 1950, Taylor led a quartet that became, under Artie Shaw's leadership, the last incarnation of Shaw's Gramercy Five. With the forming of his first trio in 1952, the polished bebop pianist's career was in full swing.

Taylor, a PhD since 1975, is convinced jazz can be taught. To prove the point, he wrote excellent pedagogical articles for *Downbeat*, *Esquire*, and *The Saturday Review of Literature*. *Jazz Piano*, his fine instructional book, is based on the thirteen-segment NPR series *Taylor Made Piano*. Very telegenic, with an appealing employee-of-the-month smile, Taylor was the musical director for David Frost's TV show (1969–72) and Arts correspondent for Charles Kuralt's *Sunday Morning* on CBS (1981). The veteran pianist has completely recovered from a recent stroke. He announced his retirement shortly thereafter.

WRAP YOUR TROUBLES IN DREAMS (AND DREAM YOUR TROUBLES AWAY)

Lyric by Ted Koehler and Billy Moll
Music by Harry Barris

Figure 57 – Head (first 8 measures)

The original sheet music key of C is replaced by B♭ for a lower and richer tonal gravitas. Chord substitutions expand the harmonic palette: A+7 on beat 3 of measure 3, and D♭9 that begins on beat 2 of measure 4. In measure 5, a pairing of Gm7 (the submediant) with D7♭9 (its dominant) is echoed with a new wrinkle: D♭9♯11.

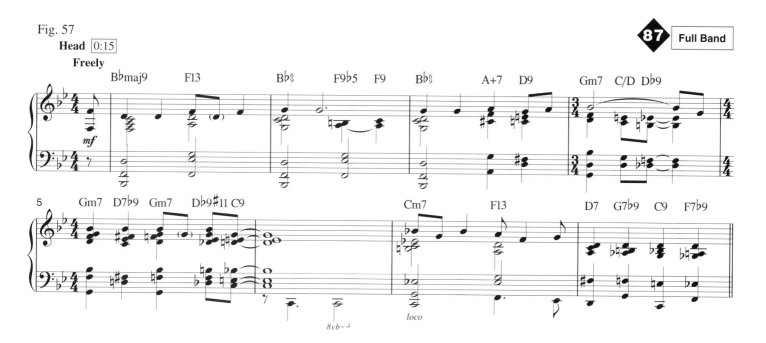

Figure 58 – Head (bridge)

Jazzmen are attracted to this section's cycle of 5ths like moths to a flame. Ubiquitous particularly in bebop, it provides the chordal sequence for the bridge of Duke Jordan's classic composition "Jordu." Taylor keeps the cycle of 5ths going even during the fills (measures 4 and 8).

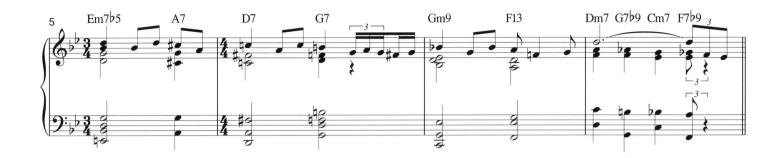

Figure 59 – First Solo Chorus (first 16 measures)

Taylor shares important common grounds with his predominant influence, Bud Powell. Taylor's attack is somewhat more restrained than his mentor's, but both pianists agree on matters of continuity, a commitment to swinging, and an ear for true jazz harmony. All those qualities are here in force.

Figure 60 – Third Solo Chorus (bridge)

The tendency to play cutesy sequential phrases over these changes is mercifully avoided. The lines are all eighth note-driven but thoughtfully melodic. Chromatic touches (measures 5 and 6) offset the generally larger intervals.

Fig. 60

Figure 61 – Recap and Ending

Three triads spar with a C pedal tone (measures 5 and 6). In measures 7–10, Taylor is headed for a big MGM-type finish. A bebop line in octave unison comes to the rescue before bathos sets in. The tonic at the extreme ends of the piano in the last measure is a good parting shot.

Fig. 61

KEYBOARD *signature licks*

These exceptional book/CD packs teach keyboardists the techniques and styles used by popular artists from yesterday and today. Each folio breaks down the trademark riffs and licks used by these great performers.

BEST OF BEBOP PIANO

by Gene Rizzo

16 bebop piano transcriptions: April in Paris • Between the Devil and the Deep Blue Sea • I Don't Stand a Ghost of a Chance • If I Were a Bell • Lullaby of Birdland • On a Clear Day (You Can See Forever) • Satin Doll • Thou Swell • and more.

00695734...$19.95

CONTEMPORARY CHRISTIAN

by Todd Lowry

Learn the trademark keyboard styles and techniques of today's top contemporary Christian artists. 12 songs, including: Fool for You (Nichole Nordeman) • The Great Divide (Point of Grace) • His Strength Is Perfect (Steven Curtis Chapman) • How Beautiful (Twila Paris) • If I Stand (Rich Mullins) • Know You in the Now (Michael Card) • and more.

00695753...$19.95

BILL EVANS

by Brent Edstrom

12 songs from pianist Bill Evans, including: Five • One for Helen • The Opener • Peace Piece • Peri's Scope • Quiet Now • Re: Person I Knew • Time Remembered • Turn Out the Stars • Very Early • Waltz for Debby • 34 Skidoo.

00695714...$22.95

BEN FOLDS FIVE

by Todd Lowry

16 songs from four Ben Folds Five albums: Alice Childress • Battle of Who Could Care Less • Boxing • Brick • Don't Change Your Plans • Evaporated • Kate • The Last Polka • Lullabye • Magic • Narcolepsy • Philosophy • Song for the Dumped • Underground.

00695578...$22.95

BILLY JOEL CLASSICS: 1974-1980

by Robbie Gennet

15 popular hits from the '70s by Billy Joel: Big Shot • Captain Jack • Don't Ask Me Why • The Entertainer • Honesty • Just the Way You Are • Movin' Out (Anthony's Song) • My Life • New York State of Mind • Piano Man • Root Beer Rag • Say Goodbye to Hollywood • Scenes from an Italian Restaurant • She's Always a Woman • The Stranger.

00695581...$22.95

BILLY JOEL HITS: 1981-1993

by Todd Lowry

15 more hits from Billy Joel in the '80s and '90s: All About Soul • Allentown • And So It Goes • Baby Grand • I Go to Extremes • Leningrad • Lullabye (Goodnight, My Angel) • Modern Woman • Pressure • The River of Dreams • She's Got a Way • Tell Her About It • This Is the Time • Uptown Girl • You're Only Human (Second Wind).

00695582...$22.95

ELTON JOHN CLASSIC HITS

by Todd Lowry

10 of Elton's best are presented in this book/CD pack: Blue Eyes • Chloe • Don't Go Breaking My Heart • Don't Let the Sun Go Down on Me • Ego • I Guess That's Why They Call It the Blues • Little Jeannie • Sad Songs (Say So Much) • Someone Saved My Life Tonight • Sorry Seems to Be the Hardest Word.

00695688...$22.95

LENNON & MCCARTNEY HITS

by Todd Lowry

Features 15 hits from A-L for keyboard by the legendary songwriting team of John Lennon and Paul McCartney. Songs include: All You Need Is Love • Back in the U.S.S.R. • The Ballad of John and Yoko • Because • Birthday • Come Together • A Day in the Life • Don't Let Me Down • Drive My Car • Get Back • Good Day Sunshine • Hello, Goodbye • Hey Jude • In My Life • Lady Madonna.

00695650...$22.95

LENNON & MCCARTNEY FAVORITES

by Todd Lowry

16 more hits (L-Z) from The Beatles: Let It Be • The Long and Winding Road • Lucy in the Sky with Diamonds • Martha My Dear • Ob-La-Di, Ob-La-Da • Oh! Darling • Penny Lane • Revolution 9 • Rocky Raccoon • She's a Woman • Strawberry Fields Forever • We Can Work It Out • With a Little Help from My Friends • The Word • You're Going to Lose That Girl • Your Mother Should Know.

00695651...$22.95

BEST OF ROCK

by Todd Lowry

12 songs are analyzed: Bloody Well Right (Supertramp) • Cold as Ice (Foreigner) • Don't Do Me Like That (Tom Petty & The Heartbreakers) • Don't Let the Sun Go Down on Me (Elton John) • I'd Do Anything for Love (Meat Loaf) • Killer Queen (Queen) • Lady Madonna (The Beatles) • Light My Fire (The Doors) • Piano Man (Billy Joel) • Point of No Return (Kansas) • Separate Ways (Journey) • Werewolves of London (Warren Zevon).

00695751...$19.95

BEST OF ROCK 'N' ROLL PIANO

by David Bennett Cohen

12 of the best hits for piano are presented in this pack. Songs include: At the Hop • Blueberry Hill • Brown-Eyed Handsome Man • Charlie Brown • Great Balls of Fire • Jailhouse Rock • Lucille • Rock and Roll Is Here to Stay • Runaway • Tutti Frutti • Yakety Yak • You Never Can Tell.

00695627...$19.95

BEST OF STEVIE WONDER

by Todd Lowry

This book/CD pack includes musical examples, lessons, biographical notes, and more for 14 of Stevie Wonder's best songs. Features: I Just Called to Say I Love You • My Cherie Amour • Part Time Lover • Sir Duke • Superstition • You Are the Sunshine of My Life • and more.

00695605...$22.95

Prices, contents and availability subject to change without notice.

0304

KEYBOARD STYLE SERIES

THE COMPLETE GUIDE WITH CD!

These book/CD packs provide focused lessons that contain valuable how-to insight, essential playing tips, and beneficial information for all players. From comping to soloing, comprehensive treatment is given to each subject. The companion CD features many of the examples in the book performed either solo or with a full band.

BEBOP JAZZ PIANO

by John Valerio

This book provides detailed information for bebop and jazz keyboardists on: chords and voicings, harmony and chord progressions, scales and tonality, common melodic figures and patterns, comping, characteristic tunes, the styles of Bud Powell and Thelonious Monk, and more. Includes 5 combo performances at the end of the book.
00290535 Book/CD Pack.....................................$17.95

BLUES PIANO

by Mark Harrison

With this book/CD pack, you'll learn the theory, the tools, and even the tricks that the pros use to play the blues. You also get seven complete tunes to jam with on the CD. Covers: scales and chords; left-hand patterns; walking bass; endings and turnarounds; right-hand techniques; how to solo with blues scales; crossover licks; and more.
00311007 Book/CD Pack.....................................$16.95

COUNTRY PIANO

by Mark Harrison

Learn the theory, the tools, and the tricks used by the pros to get that authentic country sound. This book/CD pack covers: scales and chords, walkup and walkdown patterns, comping in traditional and modern country, Nashville "fretted piano" techniques and more. At the end, you'll get to jam along with seven complete tunes.
00311052 Book/CD Pack.....................................$17.95

POST-BOP JAZZ PIANO

by John Valerio

This book/CD pack will teach you the basic skills needed to play post-bop jazz piano. Learn the theory, the tools, and the tricks used by the pros to play in the style of Bill Evans, Thelonious Monk, Herbie Hancock, McCoy Tyner, Chick Corea and others. Topics covered include: chord voicings, scales and tonality, modality, and more.
00311005 Book/CD Pack.....................................$17.95

R&B KEYBOARD

by Mark Harrison

From soul to funk to disco to pop, you'll learn the theory, the tools, and the tricks used by the pros with this book/CD pack. Topics covered include: scales and chords, harmony and voicings, progressions and comping, rhythmic concepts, characteristic stylings, the development of R&B, and more! Includes seven songs.
00310881 Book/CD Pack.....................................$17.95

ROCK KEYBOARD

by Scott Miller

Learn to comp or solo in any of your favorite rock styles. Listen to the CD to hear your parts fit in with the total groove of the band. Includes 99 tracks! Covers: classic rock, pop/rock, blues rock, Southern rock, hard rock, progressive rock, alternative rock and heavy metal.
00310823 Book/CD Pack.....................................$16.95

ROCK 'N' ROLL PIANO

by Andy Vinter

Take your place alongside Fats Domino, Jerry Lee Lewis, Little Richard, and other legendary players of the '50s and '60s! This book/CD pack covers: left-hand patterns; basic rock 'n' roll progressions; right-hand techniques; straight eighths vs. swing eighths; glisses, crushed notes, rolls, note clusters and more. Includes six complete tunes.
00310912 Book/CD Pack.....................................$16.95

SMOOTH JAZZ PIANO

by Mark Harrison

Learn the skills you need to play smooth jazz piano – the theory, the tools, and the tricks used by the pros. Topics covered include: scales and chords; harmony and voicings; progressions and comping; rhythmic concepts; melodies and soloing; characteristic stylings; discussions on jazz evolution.
00311095 Book/CD Pack.....................................$17.95

STRIDE & SWING PIANO

by John Valerio

Learn the styles of the stride and swing piano masters, such as Scott Joplin, Jimmy Yancey, Pete Johnson, Jelly Roll Morton, James P. Johnson, Fats Waller, Teddy Wilson, and Art Tatum. This book/CD pack covers classic ragtime, early blues and boogie woogie, New Orleans jazz and more. Includes 14 songs.
00310882 Book/CD Pack.....................................$17.95

Prices, contents, and availability subject to change without notice.

FOR MORE INFORMATION, SEE YOUR LOCAL MUSIC DEALER, OR WRITE TO:

HAL•LEONARD®
CORPORATION
7777 W. BLUEMOUND RD. P.O. BOX 13819 MILWAUKEE, WI 53213

Visit Hal Leonard online at
www.halleonard.com

0605

NOTE-FOR-NOTE
KEYBOARD TRANSCRIPTIONS

These outstanding collections feature note-for-note transcriptions from the artists who made the songs famous.
No matter what style you play, these books are perfect for performers or students who want to play just like their keyboard idols.

ACOUSTIC PIANO BALLADS

16 acoustic piano favorites: Angel • Candle in the Wind • Don't Let the Sun Go Down on Me • Endless Love • Imagine • It's Too Late • Let It Be • Mandy • Ribbon in the Sky • Sailing • She's Got a Way • So Far Away • Tapestry • You Never Give Me Your Money • You've Got a Friend • Your Song.

00690351 / $19.95

ELTON JOHN

18 of Elton John's best songs: Bennie and the Jets • Candle in the Wind • Crocodile Rock • Daniel • Don't Let the Sun Go Down on Me • Goodbye Yellow Brick Road • I Guess That's Why They Call It the Blues • Little Jeannie • Rocket Man • Your Song • and more!

00694829 / $19.95

THE BEATLES KEYBOARD BOOK

23 Beatles favorites, including: All You Need Is Love • Back in the U.S.S.R. • Come Together • Get Back • Good Day Sunshine • Hey Jude • Lady Madonna • Let It Be • Lucy in the Sky with Diamonds • Ob-La-Di, Ob-La-Da • Oh! Darling • Penny Lane • Revolution • We Can Work It Out • With a Little Help from My Friends • and more.

00694827 / $19.95

THE CAROLE KING KEYBOARD BOOK

16 of King's greatest songs: Beautiful • Been to Canaan • Home Again • I Feel the Earth Move • It's Too Late • Jazzman • (You Make Me Feel) Like a Natural Woman • Nightingale • Smackwater Jack • So Far Away • Sweet Seasons • Tapestry • Way Over Yonder • Where You Lead • Will You Love Me Tomorrow • You've Got a Friend.

00690554 / $19.95

CLASSIC ROCK

35 all-time rock classics: Beth • Bloody Well Right • Changes • Cold as Ice • Come Sail Away • Don't Do Me Like That • Hard to Handle • Heaven • Killer Queen • King of Pain • Layla • Light My Fire • Oye Como Va • Piano Man • Takin' Care of Business • Werewolves of London • and more.

00310940 / $24.95

POP/ROCK

35 songs, including: Africa • Against All Odds • Axel F • Centerfold • Chariots of Fire • Cherish • Don't Let the Sun Go Down on Me • Drops of Jupiter (Tell Me) • Faithfully • It's Too Late • Just the Way You Are • Let It Be • Mandy • Sailing • Sweet Dreams Are Made of This • Walking in Memphis • and more.

00310939 / $24.95

JAZZ

24 favorites from Bill Evans, Thelonious Monk, Oscar Peterson, Bud Powell, and Art Tatum and more. Includes: Ain't Misbehavin' • April in Paris • Autumn in New York • Body and Soul • Freddie Freeloader • Giant Steps • My Funny Valentine • Satin Doll • Song for My Father • Stella by Starlight • and more.

00310941 / $22.95

R&B

35 R&B classics: Baby Love • Boogie on Reggae Woman • Easy • Endless Love • Fallin' • Green Onions • Higher Ground • I'll Be There • Just Once • Money (That's What I Want) • On the Wings of Love • Ribbon in the Sky • This Masquerade • Three Times a Lady • and more.

00310942 / $24.95

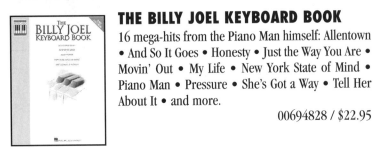

THE BILLY JOEL KEYBOARD BOOK

16 mega-hits from the Piano Man himself: Allentown • And So It Goes • Honesty • Just the Way You Are • Movin' Out • My Life • New York State of Mind • Piano Man • Pressure • She's Got a Way • Tell Her About It • and more.

00694828 / $22.95

STEVIE WONDER

14 of Stevie's most popular songs: Boogie on Reggae Woman • Hey Love • Higher Ground • I Wish • Isn't She Lovely • Lately • Living for the City • Overjoyed • Ribbon in the Sky • Send One Your Love • Superstition • That Girl • You Are the Sunshine of My Life • You Haven't Done Nothin'.

00306698 / $19.95

Prices, contents and availability subject to change without notice.

FOR MORE INFORMATION, SEE YOUR LOCAL MUSIC DEALER,
OR WRITE TO:

HAL•LEONARD®
CORPORATION
7777 W. BLUEMOUND RD. P.O. BOX 13819 MILWAUKEE, WI 53213

Visit Hal Leonard online at **www.halleonard.com**

0405